William Shakespeare's
R & J
The Concert

Teacher's Book

(CD Sold Separately)

Double Dutch Discords

DEDICATION

To all my wonderful teachers at Damascus Community School:

Mrs Mary Bitar, Mr Steve Browning, Mrs Daghestani, Mrs Jabour, Mrs Joubaily,
Mrs Cheryl Kabbarah, Mr Robert McGetchin, Mrs Moushakka, Mrs Syme,
Mrs Sultan, Mr Webber and, especially,
Mrs Helen Bachour.

CONTENTS

ACKNOWLEDGMENTS

Penny Spiers for help with editing.

INTRODUCTION

Shakespeare is not only part of our national culture & heritage, but also internationally recognized as a playwright. Shakespeare is literature at its best. It is, however, a sad acknowledgement that many may not have the opportunity to discover this national treasure because of their social, educational or linguistic background.

A 'music format' seemed an ideal choice to engage with the younger generation and it was with this in mind that we began the labour of love that the making of the CD became.

Our ultimate aim was to broaden the appeal of Shakespeare by presenting the material in an accessible format that bears more relevance for the younger generation.

The aim of this book is to provide teachers with additional supplementary material with which to engage learners in the classroom.

MUSIC & SHAKESPEARE

Music has an international appeal and incorporating it into the classroom not only adds the element of fun to the learning process but also provides a natural change of activity and pace to a lesson. In addition, the text can be enjoyed even if only partially understood.
In presenting Shakespeare in the form of songs we aim to:-

- Activate SS interest and hence inspire learning.
- Motivate SS, especially the younger generation.
- Bring the text to life and hence make it easier to remember.
- Enhance the text by providing an additional context in terms of mood and atmosphere.
- Provide SS with a relevant and understandable form that sets possibly difficult and incomprehensible language in a modern framework that invites repetition.
- Exploit a powerful learning tool that aids memory and retention.
- Effectively engage SS in coming to grips with the seemingly difficult language via collaborative activities.
- Exploit the text by incorporating multi-skills activities [reading/writing/listening/speaking].
- Provide further classroom practice to highlight the timeless relevance of Shakespeare's words.

HOW TO USE IN THE CLASSROOM

Mainstream, as part of an English Literature course/examination:
This is a resource book for teachers to use as supplementary material to the relevant course/examination materials. Learning Shakespeare can be arduous and frustrating for many learners, mainly due to the archaic language. This book serves to inject the classroom with bursts of motivation, interest and enjoyment, as and when required by the teacher. It provides a natural change of activity and pace in a lesson and adds an element of fun to the learning process. The exercises are aimed at exploiting the text to the full, with the premise that learners are already familiar with some Shakespearean texts.

English as a Foreign Language learner: Advanced
This is a resource book for teachers to use in supplementary/extra classes for full-time, live-in courses. There is a chronic need for more resource books that exploit works of literature and the fact that learners themselves enjoy works of literature is precisely because the authors are internationally renowned. The sense of achievement at having managed to comprehend works of literature is tremendously satisfying and confidence boosting for learners. Shakespeare is a natural choice as he is an internationally known playwright.

Please note, this resource book is not intended for EFL (Cambridge) examination courses.

Although, primarily aimed at Advanced learners, the book could also be used at Upper Intermediate levels if care is taken in selection of text and exercise.

ORGANISATION

- The book itself is based on a CD of songs. There are a total of 22 songs, all of which cover the main events in Romeo & Juliet: the Play. The words/text itself are Shakespeare word for word. The book is easy to use and can be photocopied. The book is indexed in line with song titles on the CD.

- The main exercises are 'Gap-fill' activities, 'Text Ordering' activities and 'Complete the Sentences' activities. All activities are multi-skill, involve reading, listening, speaking and writing and demand active learner participation.
  Please refer to the relevant Guidance Notes provided for each type of activity.

- Additional discussion points, which can be done in pairs or groups depending on class size, are provided for some songs.

- A suggested Lesson Plan Guide is also provided, which can be adapted/docked according to the learners' level/needs.

Shakespeare-Speak

Shakespeare-Speak is an optional section at the end of the book, the aim of which is to familiarize learners with the basic and common archaic forms that they are likely to come across in the text in a free and fun way. It is best to introduce learners to the text via some form of similar activity prior to embarking upon the main exercises.

The Songs

We have incorporated an eclectic range of musical styles on the CD so as not to limit its scope in any way.

The songs may at first listening seem difficult and lacking in clarity due to the intrinsic nature of pop songs. For reasons of authenticity, we have chosen not to alter the songs for the purposes of a listening exercise. Accompanying exercises, whether gap-fills or text-ordering, all serve to provide learners with adequate information.

1. Read the text quickly: How many hours does the play last?
2. Replace the definitions with Shakespeare's own words [in the box].
3. In pairs, compare your answers.
4. Complete and check your answers.

Star-crossed	civil	toil	strife
~~households~~	passage	mutiny	From forth
misadventur'd	nought	rage	lay

Definitions

Two __households__ both alike in dignity,   families
[In fair Verona where we _____ our scene]   set
From ancient *grudge**, break to new _____ ,   violence
Where civil blood makes _____ hands unclean;   citizens'
_____ _____ the fatal loins of these two foes,   Produced from
A pair of _____ lovers, take their life: unlucky
Whose _____ piteous *overthrows**,   unfortunate
Doth with their death bury their parents' _____ .   conflict
The fearful _____ of their death-mark'd love,   course
And the continuance of their parents' _____: anger
Which *but** their children's end _____ could remove: nothing
Is now the two hours' traffic of our Stage.
The which if you with patient ears attend,
What here shall miss, our _____ shall *strive** to mend.   hard work

* *grudge:* quarrel
* *overthrows:* disasters
* *but:* except for
* *strive:* aim

01B   Prologue [Chorus]
Discussion

1.   Do you think the Prologue is necessary? Why? Why not?

_____

2.   If you were Shakespeare, would you have included the Prologue? Why? Why not?

_____

3.   List the pros and cons of holding grudges.

_____
_____
_____
_____
_____

4.   Do you hold grudges or easily forget and forgive?

_____
_____

5.   Sometimes, it's good to hold grudges. Discuss.

_____

6.   Is it right to pass on grudges on to the next generation?

_____
_____
_____

7.   Some wounds run too deep to be healed. Do you agree/disagree?

_____
_____

8.   Do you agree with Alexander Pope that: _To err is human, to forgive divine._

_____
_____

9.   Do you agree with Malachy McCourt that: _Holding a grudge is like drinking poison and then hoping the other person dies._

_____
_____
_____

The Prince of Verona (Escales)   [Act I, Scene 1]

1. Read the text quickly: When does Montague have to see the Prince?
2. Replace the definitions with Shakespeare's own words [in the box].
3. In pairs, compare your answers.
4. Listen. Complete and check your answers.

mistemper'd	forfeit	thrice	issuing
common	moved	~~Profaners~~	brawls
pernicious	pleasure	To wield	Cast by

Definitions

Rebellious Subjects enemies to peace,
  Profaners of this *neighbour-stained steel**,   abusers
Will they not hear? What ho, you men, you beasts:
That quench the fire of your _____ rage,   harmful
With purple fountains _____ from your veins: flowing out
On pain of torture from those bloody hands,
Throw your _____ weapons to the ground,   misused
And hear the sentence of your _____ Prince.   angry
Three civil _____ *bred of airy word**,   fights
By thee old Capulet and Montague,
Have _____ disturb'd the quiet of our streets,   three times
And made Verona's ancient citizens,
_____ their *grave beseeming ornaments**,   Throw aside
_____ old *partisans, in hands as old**,   To hold
Canker'd* with peace, to part your canker'd hate.
If ever you disturb our streets again,
Your lives shall pay the _____ of the peace.   penalty
For this time all the rest depart away:
You Capulet shall go along with me,
And Montague come you this afternoon,
To know our farther _____ in this case: decision
To old Free-town, our _____ judgement place: public
Once more on pain of death, all men depart.

* *neighbour-stained steel:* weapons stained with neighbour's blood
* *bred of airy word:* produced by some casual remark
* *grave beseeming ornaments:* sensible ornaments of peaceful life
* *partisans, in hands as old:* supporters, in hands as old as the weapons
* *Canker'd:* Rusty/Spoilt

02B   Rebellious Subjects [Act I, Scene 1]
Discussion

1.   What words in the text do you think best reflect the Prince's anger and outrage? List.

Discuss together and narrow them down to 5 words: _____

2.   Do you think the Prince is right in his anger and outrage? Why/Why not?

3.   If you were the Prince, what would you do to ensure that both sides stopped fighting?

4.   If you were the head of a country, i.e., Prime Minister or President, what things would make you angry? How would you solve the problem?

5.   *If ever you disturb our streets again, your lives shall pay the forfeit of the peace'.*
     Do you agree with him? Why? Why not?

6.   List the pros and cons of capital punishment.

7.   Do you think the music complemented the text? Why? Why not?
     How would you have done it?

Romeo and Benvolio   [Act I, Scene 2]

1.   Read the text and decide who is speaking.
2.   Complete the box: match words and meanings.
3.   Place the words in **bold** [in the box] into the text.
4.   In pairs, compare your answers.
5.   Listen. Complete and check your answers.

Maintains	unprejudiced	**pois'd with**	equal
devout	a black bird	**match**	hardly
unattainted	believes	**splendour**	non-believers
feast	dines	**rejoice**	beauty
crow	party	**scant**	be happy
Sups	deeply felt	**heretics**	balanced against

_____: At this same ancient _____ of Capulet's.
               _____ the fair Rosalind whom thou so loves:
               With all the admired beauties of Verona,
               Go thither, and with _____ eye,
               Compare her face with some that I shall show,
               And I will make thee think thy swan a _____.

_____: When the _____ religion of mine eye,
                 **Maintains** such falsehood, then turn tears to fires:
               And these who often drown'd, could never die,
               Transparent _____ be burnt for liars.
               One fairer than my love, the all-seeing Sun,
               Ne'er saw her _____, since first the world begun.

_____: Tut you saw her fair none else being by,
               Herself _____ _____ herself in either eye:
               But in that crystal scales let there be weigh'd,
               Your lady's love against some other maid:
               That I will show you shining at this feast,
               And she shall _____ show well that now seems best.

_____: I'll go along no such sight to be shown,
               But to _____ in _____ of mine own.

03B   The Feast of Capulet [Act I, Scene 2]
Discussion

1.   List all words/phrases in the text that relate to the eyes:

_____

_____

_____

Why do you think the 'eyes' are important in the story of 'love'?

_____

_____

2.   *'And these who often drown'd, …'*
What do you think 'these' refers to?   _____

What do you think 'drown'd' means here?   _____

'Transparent heretics be burnt for liars.'
What do you think 'Transparent heretics' refers to?   _____

3.   *'But in that crystal scales let there be weigh'd,…'*
What do you think 'crystal scales' refers to?   _____

4.   Why do you think *eyes* are described as 'transparent' and 'crystal' in the text?

_____

_____

5.   Do you think Romeo falls in love too easily? Why/Why not?

_____

6.   Do you think Benvolio is right in saying that Romeo should 'compare' Rosalind to 'some other maid'? Why/Why not?

_____

_____

7.   If you were Romeo's friend, would you give him the same advice? Why? Why not?

_____

_____

8.   Do you agree with the following? Give your reasons.
(a)   'Eyes are the windows of the soul'   _____
(b)   'Beauty is in the eye of the beholder'   _____
(c)   'Love is blind'   _____

Romeo and Juliet

Read each pair of sentences and match the underlined words with their definitions below:-

(c)   1. He profaned the religion by wearing his shoes in the Mosque.
          You must not profane the Lord's name.

_____   2. When you get christened, the priest uses holy water.
          In Buddhism, cows are considered as holy.

_____   3. Mecca is a shrine for Muslims.
          She loved Elvis so much, that her bedroom was a shrine to him.

_____   4. Millions of pilgrims travelled to Rome for the Pope's funeral.
          Pilgrims from all around the world travel to Mecca.

_____   5. Mother Theresa of Calcutta should have been made a saint.
          Saint Christopher is the patron saint who protects travellers.

_____   6. Theft is considered a sin in most religions.
          She treats being late for meals as an unforgivable sin.

_____   7. To purge her conscience, she's decided to give money to charities.
          She went abroad in order to purge all her unpleasant memories.

_____   8. He had trespassed by reading her diary.
          Forgive our trespasses as we forgive those who trespass against us.

          (a)   associated with God or religion
          (b)   to purify/to cleanse oneself from something bad or undesirable
          (c)   **to treat a sacred thing with lack of respect**
          (d)   a place that is regarded as holy
          (e)   a person who's regarded as holy by the Christian church because of
                his/her good works or qualities
          (f)   a person who travels to a holy place for religious reasons
          (g)   to do wrong; to break a religious or moral law
          (h)   a crime; an offence against a religious or moral law

1.   In groups brainstorm: *Religions* [types of, countries, associated words, etc]
2.   In groups/pairs, put the dialogue in order.
3.   Listen. Complete & check.

A	**Romeo:** O the dear Saint, let lips do what hands do, They pray, grant thou, lest faith turn to despair.
B	**Juliet:** Good Pilgrim you do wrong your hands too much Which mannerly devotion shows in this, For saints have hands, that Pilgrims' hand do touch, And palm to palm is holy *Palmer's* kiss. *pilgrims*
C	**Romeo:** Then move not while my prayer's effect I take, Thus from my lips, by thine my sin is purg'd.
D	**Juliet:** Then have my lips the sin that they have took.
E	**Romeo:** If I profane with my unworthiest hand, This holy shrine, the gentle sin is this, My lips two blushing Pilgrims ready stand, To smooth the rough touch with a gentle kiss.
F	**Juliet:** Saints do not move, though grant for prayers' sake.
G	**Romeo:** Sin from my lips, O trespass sweetly urg'd: Give me my sin again.
H	**Juliet:** Ay Pilgrim, lips that they must use in prayer.
I	**Romeo:** Have not Saints lips and holy *Palmers* too?

1.   In this first meeting between Romeo and Juliet, where they flirt with each other, a lot of religious metaphors are used. List as many as you can find:

_____

_____

_____

Why do you think Shakespeare used so many religious references in this love scene? _____

_____

Do you think the religious metaphors used by Romeo and Juliet in their flirtations are appropriate? Why? Why not? _____

_____

2.   *'If I profane with my unworthiest hand,*
      This holy shrine, the gentle sin is this,'
      What do you think 'this holy shrine' refers to? _____

3.   *'Which mannerly devotion shows in this,'*
      'Which mannerly devotion' means 'which shows proper respect in what it is doing'. What do you think Juliet is referring to by 'this'? _____

_____

4.   *'O dear saint, let lips do what hands do'*
      What do you think Romeo means? _____

_____

5.   *'Then move not while my prayer's effect I take'*
      What do you think he means by 'my prayer's effect'? _____

6.   Romeo kisses Juliet twice in this scene. Discuss and decide at which point he kisses her and why you think so. _____

_____

_____

7.   Do you think that 'love' is a religious experience? Why? Why not?

_____

_____

_____

9

05A   JULIET IS THE SUN
[Act II, Scene 2]

1.   Read the text and decide who is speaking.
2.   Put the words [in the box] into the text.
3.   In pairs, compare your answers.
4.   Listen. Complete and check your answers.

fools	envious	East	pale	~~light~~
speaks	answer	moon	Lady	nothing

Box A

A   But soft, what __light__ through yonder window breaks?
It is the _____, and Juliet is the Sun.
Arise fair sun and kill the envious _____,
Who is already sick and _____ with grief,
That thou her maid art far more fair than she:
Be not her maid since she is _____,
Her *vestal livery** is but sick and green,
And none but _____ do wear it, cast it off:
It is my _____, O it is my love,
O that she knew she were,
She speaks, yet she says _____, what of that?
Her eye *discourses**, I will _____ it:
I am too bold, 'tis not to me she _____:

bright	eyes	daylight	birds	~~heaven~~
glove	cheek	touch	twinkle	brightness

Box B

B   Two of the fairest stars in all the __heaven__,
Having some business do intreat her _____,
To _____ in their spheres till they return.
What if her eyes were there, they in her head,
The _____ of her cheek would shame those stars
As _____ doth a lamp, her eye in heaven
Would through the *airy region** stream so _____,
That _____ would sing, and think it were not night:
See how she leans her _____ upon her hand.
O that I were a _____ upon that hand,
That I might _____ that cheek.

* *vestal livery:* virginal attire/clothes
* *discourses:* speaks
* *airy region:* sky

10

Juliet   [Act II, Scene 2]

1. In groups brainstorm: *What's in a name?*
2. In groups/pairs, put Juliet's words in order.
3. Listen. Complete and check your order.

A	Take all my self.
B	And I'll no longer be a Capulet.
C	What's in a name? That which we call a rose,
D	Retain that dear perfection which he *owes*, *owns*
E	What's Montague? It is nor hand nor foot,
F	Belonging to a man. O be some other name.
G	Without that title, Romeo doff thy name,
H	Thou art thyself, though not a Montague,
I	Deny thy father and refuse thy name.
J	*Romeo: Shall I hear more, or shall I speak at this?*
K	O Romeo, Romeo, wherefore art thou Romeo?
L	'Tis but thy name that is my enemy:
M	By any other name would smell as sweet,
N	And for thy name which is no part of thee,
O	So Romeo would were he not Romeo call'd
P	Nor arm nor face, nor any other part
Q	Or if thou wilt not, be sworn my love,

Discussion

1.   Transcribe the following into modern English:
     'Romeo, wherefore art thou Romeo?' _____
     'Retain that dear perfection which he owes,' _____
     'Romeo doff thy name' _____
     _____

2.   Are names really important? Why? Why not? _____
     _____
     _____

3.   Would you still be 'you' if you had a different name? _____
     _____
     _____

4.   If you could change your name, what would you change it to? Why?
     _____

5.   Would you still be 'you'
     … if you had different colour skin? _____
     … if you had different religion? _____
     … if were from a different country? _____

6.   Would you be willing to change your name for 'love'? Why? Why not?
     _____

7.   Under what circumstances would you be willing to change your name? Why?
     _____
     _____

8.   Girls normally take on their husband's family name when they get married.
     Why do you think that is so? Do you think it's a good/fair thing? Why?
     Why not?
     _____
     _____
     _____

9.   Would you be happy to change your family name when you marry? Why?
     Why not?
     _____

Friar Laurence, Romeo, Juliet   [Act II, Scene 6]

1. Read the text quickly: What is 'this holy act'?
2. In pairs, read the text carefully and decide who is speaking.
3. Listen. Complete and check your answers.

_____ : So smile the heavens upon this holy act,
That *after hours* with sorrow *chide* us not.   *in times to come/ blame*

_____ : Amen, amen, but come what sorrow can,
It cannot *countervail* the exchange of joy   *equal*
That one short minute gives me in her sight:
Do thou but close our hands with holy words,
Then love-devouring death do what he dare,
It is enough I may but call her mine.

_____ : These violent delights have violent ends,
And in their triumph die like fire and *powder:*   *gun powder*
Which as they kiss consume. The sweetest honey
Is loathsome in his own deliciousness,
And in their taste *confounds* the appetite.   *ruins*
Therefore, love moderately, long love doth so,
Too swift arrives, as *tardy* as too slow.   *slack*

Here comes the Lady. Oh so light a foot
Will ne'er wear out the everlasting *flint,*   *cobble stones*
A lover may *bestride* the *gossamers,*   *ride upon/ webs*
That *idles* in the *wanton* summer air,   *floats/ playful*
And yet not fall, so light is vanity.

_____ : Good even to my *ghostly* confessor.   *spiritual*
_____ : Romeo shall thank thee daughter for us both.
_____ : As much to him, else in his thanks too much.
_____ : Ah, Juliet, if the measure of thy joy
Be heap'd like mine, and that thy skill be more
To *blazon* it, then sweeten with thy breath   *proclaim*
This *neighbour* air, and let rich music's tongue   *shared*
Unfold the imagin'd happiness that both   *express*
Receive *in either*, by this dear encounter.   *in each other*

_____ : *Conceit* more rich in matter than in words,   *a (fanciful) thought*
Brags of his substance, not of ornament:
They are but beggars that can count their worth,
But my true love is grown to such excess,
I cannot sum up *sum* of half my wealth.   *the total amount*

_____ : Come, come with me, and we will make short work.
For by your leaves, you shall not stay alone,
Till holy Church *incorporate* two in one.   *Join*

Discussion

1.   Why do you think the Friar says:-
      'That after hours with sorrow chide us not'?   _____
      'These violent delights have violent ends'?   _____

2.   *'Therefore, love moderately, long love doth so,*
      Too swift arrives, as tardy as too slow.'
      The Friar advises them to love moderately for long lasting love.
      What do you think he means by: *'Too swift arrives, as tardy as too slow.'*?
      _____

      Do you agree with the Friar? Why/Why not?   _____
      _____

3.   *'Unfold the imagin'd happiness that both*
      Receive in either, by this dear encounter.'
      What does 'this dear encounter' refer to?   _____

4.   Where in the text do you think Juliet enters and embraces Romeo?
      _____

      What do you think the following lines indicate:-
      Friar: *'Romeo shall thank thee daughter for us both'*   _____
      Juliet: *'As much to him, else in his thanks too much.'*   _____

5.   *'Conceit more rich in matter than in words.'*
      What do you think 'Conceit' refers to: _____

6.   What lines in the text do you think reflects the following statements:-
      (a) 'Actions speak louder than words'   _____
      _____
      (b) 'Only the poor can count how much they have.'   _____
      _____

      Do you agree with the above statements? Why/Why not?
      _____
      _____

7.   Do you think Romeo and Juliet are wrong in 'rushing' into marriage? Why?
      Why not?   _____

8.   What do you think is the 'ideal' age to get married? Give your reasons.
      _____

Romeo, Mercutio, Benvolio   [Act III, Scene 1]

1. In groups/pairs a) put the text in order and b) decide who is speaking.
2. Listen. Complete and check your answers.

A _____:	Help me into some house Benvolio, Or I shall faint, a plague a'both your houses. They have made *worms' meat* of me, I have it, and soundly, to your houses.	*dead body*
B _____:	Courage man, the hurt cannot be much.	
C	*<Tybalt under Romeo's arm thrusts Mercutio in; and flies>*	
D _____:	Ay, ay, a scratch, a scratch, marry t'is enough Where is my page? Go villain, fetch a surgeon.	
E _____:	What art thou hurt?	
F _____:	Draw Benvolio, beat down their weapons: Gentlemen, for shame *forbear* this outrage, Tybalt, Mercutio, the Prince expressly hath Forbid this *bandying* in Verona street, Hold Tybalt, good Mercutio.	*stop* *fighting*
G _____:	I am hurt. A plague o'both houses, I am *sped*: Is he gone and hath *nothing*?	*done for* *no wound*
H _____:	I thought all for the best.	
I _____:	No 'tis not so deep as a well, nor so wide as a churchdoor, but 'tis enough, 'twill *serve*: ask for me tomorrow, and you shall find me a grave man. I am *peppered* I warrant, for this world, a plague a'both your houses, 'zounds, a dog, a rat, a mouse, a cat, to scratch a man to death: a braggart, a rogue a villain, that fights by the book of arithmetic, why the devil came you between us? I was hurt under your arm.	*to kill me* *finished*

08B   A Plague on Both Houses [Act III, Scene 1]
Discussion

1.   Why do you think Romeo was so keen to stop the fighting at the start?

2.   Do you think Romeo was right in trying to stop the fight at the start? Why?
      Why not?

3.   Would you describe Romeo's behaviour as cowardly? Why/Why not?

4.   If you saw a fight that was about to start, would you....
      (a)   encourage the fight?
      (b)   join the fight?
      (c)   try to stop the fight?
      (d)   go and find/call the police?
      (e)   walk away?
      (f)   record it & post it on YouTube?

      Give your reasons.

5.   Would you describe Tybalt as brave or as a coward? Give your reasons.

6.   *'I was hurt under your arm'*
      Do you think Mercutio was right in 'blaming' Romeo's behaviour for his fatal
      wound? Why? Why not?

7.   *'A plague a' both your houses'.*
      What do you think Mercutio means by that?

Romeo, Benvolio, Tybalt   [Act III, Scene 1]

1. In groups/pairs a) put the text in order and b) decide who is speaking.
2. Listen. Complete and check your answers.

A ____ :	O Romeo, Romeo, brave Mercutio is dead, That gallant spirit hath *aspir'd* the clouds, Which too *untimely* here did scorn the earth.	*gone up to* *soon*
B ____ :	He gone in triumph, and Mercutio slain? Away to heaven, *respective lenity*, And fire and fury, be my *conduct* now. Now Tybalt take the villain back again, That late thou gav'st me, for Mercutio's soul Is but little way above our heads, *Staying* for thine to keep him company: Either thou or I, or both, must go with him.	*considerate mercy* *guide* *waiting*
C	*<They fight. Tybalt falls.>*	
D ____ :	This gentleman, the Prince's near *ally*, My very friend hath got this *mortal hurt* In my behalf, my reputation stain'd With Tybalt's *slander*, Tybalt that an hour Hath been my cousin: O sweet Juliet Thy beauty hath made me effeminate, And in my temper soften'd *valour steel*.	*family relation* *deadly wound* *insults* *steely courage*
E ____ :	Here comes the furious Tybalt back again.	
F ____ :	Thou wretched boy that didst *consort* him here, Shalt with him hence.	*accompany*
G ____ :	This day's black fate, on moe days doth depend; This but begins, the *woe* others must end.	*sadness*
H ____ :	This shall determine that.	
I ____ :	O I am fortune's *fool*.	*play thing*
J ____ :	Romeo, away be gone: The citizens are *up*, and Tybalt slain, Stand not amaz'd, the Prince will *doom thee* death, If thou art taken, hence be gone away.	*awake* *condemn you to*

Discussion

1.   *'O sweet Juliet, thy beauty hath made me effeminate'*
     What do you think Romeo means by that? _____
     _____
     _____

2.   Upon hearing about Mercutio's death, Romeo is determined to avenge
     Mercutio's death. What words/lines reflect Romeo's determination?
     _____
     _____
     _____
     _____

3.   Do you think Romeo was right to kill Tybalt in revenge? Why/Why not?
     _____
     _____

4.   If your friend was killed, would you avenge his/her death? Why/Why not?
     _____
     _____

5.   Do you think revenge/violence solves problems or adds to them? Why?
     Why not?
     _____
     _____

6.   Do you agree with the following? Why/Why not?
     'An eye for an eye, a tooth for a tooth' _____
     'Turn the other cheek' _____

7.   'An eye for an eye will only make the whole world blind.' - *Gandhi*
     Do you agree? Why/Why not?
     _____
     _____

8.   You should never act in anger. Do you agree? Why/Why not?
     _____
     _____

9.   Why do you think Romeo says: *'O I am fortune's fool'?*
     _____
     _____

1.   Read the text and decide who is speaking.
2.   In pairs discuss and complete the sentences in your own words (_____).
3.   Listen to see if your sentences are close to the actual words.
4.   Listen and complete with Shakespeare's words (.........).

Come night, come Romeo, come thou _____ / ....

Come gentle night, come loving _____ / ....

Give me my Romeo, and when he _____ / ....

Take him and cut him _____ / ....

And he will make the face of heaven _____ / ....

That all the world will _____ / ....

O I have bought the mansion _____ / ....

But not possess'd it, and though I am _____ / ....

Not yet _____ / ....

Check what you have written.

> Come night, come Romeo, come thou day in night
>
> Come gentle night, come loving black-brow'd night
> Give me my Romeo, and when he shall die,
> Take him and cut him out in little stars,
> And he will make the face of heaven so fine,
> That all the world will be in love with night
>
> O I have bought the mansion of a love,
> But not possess'd it, and though I am sold,
> Not yet enjoy'd

11A   BACK FOOLISH TEARS
[Act III, Scene 2]

1. Read the text quickly and decide who is speaking.
2. Refer to text and complete the matching exercise [box 1].
3. Put the words in **bold** [in box 2] into the text.
4. Listen. Complete and check your answers.

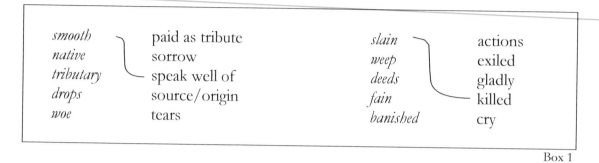

smooth	paid as tribute
native	sorrow
tributary	speak well of
drops	source/origin
woe	tears

slain	actions
weep	exiled
deeds	gladly
fain	killed
banished	cry

Box 1

Tybalt [x6]   **Romeo** [x1]   **lord** [x1]
husband [x4]   **cousin** [x2]   **wife** [x1]

Box 2

Shall I speak ill of him that is my   __husband__ ?
Ah poor my _____, what tongue shall *smooth* thy name,
When I thy three-hours _____ have mangled it?
But wherefore villain didst thou kill my _____?
That villain _____ would have kill'd my _____:
Back foolish tears, back to your *native* spring,
Your *tributary drops* belong to *woe*,
Which you mistaking offer up to joy:
My _____ lives that _____ would have *slain*,
And _____'s dead that would have slain my _____:
All this is comfort, wherefore *weep* I then?
Some word there was, worser than _____'s death
That murder'd me, I would forget it *fain*,
But Oh it presses to my memory,
Like damned guilty *deeds* to sinners' minds,
_____ is dead and _____ *banished*:
That banished, that one word banished,
Hath slain ten thousand _____: _____'s death
Was *woe* enough if it had ended there:

Romeo

1. Complete the matching exercise [in the box].
2. Put Romeo's words in order.
3. Listen. Complete and check your order.

purgatory	outside
without	forgiveness
torture	movement of the arm
banished	misnamed
stroke	causing strong pain as punishment
mis-term'd	exiled/sent away from one' original country as punishment
mercy	place where souls of dead people are made to suffer to cleanse them ready for heaven [R Catholic religion]

A	Thou cut'st my head off with a golden axe,
B	'Tis torture and not mercy, heaven is here
C	There is no world without Verona walls,
D	Where Juliet lives, and every cat and dog,
E	But Romeo may not.
F	Is death, mis-term'd, calling death banished,
G	Hence banished, is banish'd from the world
H	And little mouse, every unworthy thing
I	But purgatory, torture, hell itself:
J	Live here in heaven, and may look on her,
K	And world's exile is death. Then banished
L	And smilest upon the stroke that murders me.

13A THERE ART THOU HAPPY
[Act III, Scene 3]

1. Read the text quickly and decide who is speaking.
2. Refer to text and complete the matching exercise [box 1].
3. Put the words in **bold** [in box 2] into the text.
4. Listen. Complete and check your answers.

Box 1

denote	balanced
unseemly	to make angry
disposition	kill
temper'd	nature
slay/slew/slain	indicate/show
rouse	improper

Box 2

womanish	~~hand~~
Tybalt	**Lady**
kill	**man**
beast	**happy**
Juliet	**thyself**

Hold thy desperate   **hand** :
Art thou a _____? Thy form cries out thou art:
Thy tears are _____, thy wild acts *denote*
The unreasonable fury of a _____.
Unseemly woman in a seeming man,
And ill-beseeming beast in seeming both,
Thou hast amaz'd me. By my holy order,
I thought thy *disposition* better *temper'd*.
Hast thou *slain* _____? Wilt thou *slay* thyself?
And *slay* thy _____, that in thy life lives,
By doing damned hate upon _____?

What *rouse* thee man, thy _____ is alive,
For whose dear sake thou wast but lately dead.
There art thou happy: Tybalt would _____ thee,
But thou slew'st Tybalt: there are thou _____.

1.   What do you think happened just before this scene that made the Friar say:
     '*Hold thy desperate hand:*'

     _____

2.   '*Unseemly woman in a seeming man,*
     And ill-beseeming beast in seeming both transcribes to:
     'Improper behaviour for a woman in someone who seems like a man
     and a horrible beast in both a man and a woman'
     What behaviour do you think the Friar is referring to?

     _____

     _____

3.   What do you think the Friar means by: '*By doing damned hate upon thyself?*'

     _____

4.   Do you think Romeo's behaviour is honourable or cowardly, given his
     circumstances? Why?

     _____

     _____

5.   Do you think the Friar is right in being angry/disappointed with Romeo's
     behaviour? Why/Why not?

     _____

     _____

6.   Find examples in the text that reflects the Friar's sentiments:

     _____

     _____

     _____

7.   Do you agree with the Friar that Romeo should be happy and grateful given
     his present circumstances? Why/Why not?

     _____

     _____

     _____

8.   Do you agree with the following sayings? Give your reasons.
     'Every cloud has a silver lining'   _____
     'Be grateful for what you have'   _____

[Act III, Scene 5]   Romeo and Juliet

1.   In groups/pairs a) put the text in order and b) decide who is speaking.
2.   Listen. Complete and check your answers.

A _____ : Let me be *ta'en*, let me be put to death, I am content, so thou wilt have it so. I'll say yon grey is not the morning's eye 'Tis but the pale *reflex* of Cynthia's *brow*. Nor that is not the lark whose notes do beat The vaulty heaven so high above our heads, I have more care to stay, than will to go: Come death and welcome, Juliet wills it so. How is't my soul? Let's talk, it is not day.	*taken* *reflection / face*
B _____ : Yond light is not daylight, I know it I: It is some meteor that the Sun exhales, To be to thee this night a torch-bearer, And light thee on thy way to Mantua. Therefore stay yet, thou needs not to be gone.	
C _____ : It was the lark, the *herald* of the morn: No nightingale: look love what envious streaks Do lace the *severing* clouds in yonder East: Night's candles are burnt out, and *jocund* day Stands tiptoe on the misty mountain tops, I must be gone and live, or stay and die.	*announcer* *parting* *cheerful*
D _____ : Wilt thou be gone? It is not yet near day: It was the *nightingale*, and not the *lark*, The pierc'd the fearful hollow of thine ear, Nightly she sings on yond pomegranate tree, Believe me love, it was the nightingale.	*types of birds*

14B   Discussion

1.   '*'Tis but the pale reflex of Cynthia's bow*'. What do you think 'Cynthia' refers to?
2.   Why do you think Romeo will die if he stays?
3.   If in staying Romeo dies, why does Juliet encourage him to stay?
4.   What do you think Juliet says in the next scene after Romeo agrees to stay?

1.   Read the text and decide who is speaking.
2.   In pairs, discuss and complete the sentences in your own words (_____).
3.   Listen to see if your sentences are close to the actual words.
4.   Listen and complete with Shakespeare's words (........).

Hang thee young baggage, disobedient _____ / ....

I tell thee what, get thee to _____ / ....

Or never after look _____ / ....

Speak not, reply not, do not _____ / ....

My fingers itch, wife: we scarce thought us _____ / ....

That God had lent us but this only _____ / ....

But now I see this one is _____ / ....

And that we have a curse in _____ / ....

Out on her, *hilding*.   [*Worthless creature*]

Check what you have written.

Hang thee young *baggage*, disobedient wretch,   *woman of lax morals* I tell thee what, get thee to church a"Thursday, Or never after look me in the face. Speak not, reply not, do not answer me. My fingers itch, wife: we scarce thought us blest, That God had lent us but this only child, But now I see this one is one too much, And that we have a curse in having her: Out on her, *hilding*.   *Worthless creature*

15B   I Will Not Marry Paris [Act III, Scene 5]
Discussion

1.   Who has Juliet's father arranged for her to marry? _____

2.   As an only child, do you think greater demands and expectations are placed upon Juliet? _____
_____

3.   *'My fingers itch, wife:'*
      What do you think he means? _____
_____

4.   Do you think that children should do as they are told? Why/Why not?
_____
_____

5.   Do you think Juliet's father is right in making Juliet marry? Why/Why not?
_____
_____

6.   Do you agree with 'arranged' marriages? Why? Why not?
_____
_____
_____

7.   Why do you think people 'arranged' marriages in the past?
_____
_____

8.   If you were Juliet, what would you do? Why? _____
_____

9.   In groups, transcribe the text into modern day language:

_____
_____
_____
_____
_____
_____
_____
_____
_____

Friar Laurence

1. Read the text quickly: Where will Romeo take Juliet?
2. Put the words [in the box] into the text.
3. In pairs, compare your answers.
4. Listen. Complete and check your answers.

Bridegroom	death	letters	free	~~home~~
marry	drink	robes	bed	run
Nurse	cold	waking	alone	breath
cheeks	forty	shame	sleep	ashes

Hold then, go __home__ , be merry, give *consent*,   *agreement*

To _____ Paris: Wednesday is tomorrow,

To-morrow night *look* that thou lie _____,   *see to it*

Let not the _____ lie with thee in thy chamber:

Take thou this *vial*, being then in bed,   *small container*

And this distilled liquor _____ thou off,

When presently through all thy veins shall _____,

A _____ and drowsy *humour*: for no pulse   *sensation*

Shall keep his native *progress* but *surcease*,   *movement / stop*

No warmth, no _____ shall testify thou livest,

The roses in thy lips and _____ shall fade

To many _____, thy *eyes' windows* fall: *eye lids*

Like death when he shuts up the day of life:

Each part depriv'd of *supple government*,   *power of movement*

Shall stiff and stark, and cold appear like _____,

And in this *borrow'd* likeness of shrunk death   *false*

Thou shalt continue two and _____ hours,

And then awake as from a pleasant _____.

Now when the _____ in the morning comes,

To *rouse* thee from thy _____, there art thou dead: *wake*

Then as the *manner* of our country is,   *custom*

In thy best _____ uncovered on the *bier*,   *coffin*

Be borne to burial in thy *kindred's* grave: *relatives'*

Thou shalt be *borne* to that same ancient vault,   *carried*

Where all the kindred of the Capulet's lie;

In the mean time *against* thou shalt awake,   *ready for*

Shall Romeo by my _____ know our *drift*,   *plan*

And hither shall he come, and he and I

Will watch thy _____, and that very night

Shall Romeo *bear* thee hence to Mantua.   *take*

And this shall _____ thee from this present _____.

[Act IV, Scene 3]   Juliet

1.   In groups discuss: *Would you fake you own death? Why/Why not?*
2.   In groups/pairs, put the text in order.
3.   Listen. Complete and check your answers.

A	My *dismal scene* I needs must act alone. Come *vial*, what if this mixture do not work at all? Shall I be married then to-morrow morning?	*dreadful situation* *small container*
B	I fear it is, and yet me thinks it should not, For he hath *still been tried* a holy man. How if when I am laid into the *tomb*, I wake before the time that Romeo	*always been found* *grave*
C	Romeo, Romeo, Romeo, here's drink, I drink to thee.	
D	No, no this shall forbid it, lie thou there. <*Laying down her dagger*> What if it be a poison which the Friar	
E	Come to *redeem* me, there's a fearful point: Shall I not then be stifled in the vault?	*rescue*
F	That almost freezes up the heat of life: I'll call them back again to comfort me. Nurse, what should she do here?	
G	Farewell, God knows when we shall meet again. I have a faint cold fear *thrills* through my veins,	*shivers*
H	Subtly hath *minister'd* to have me dead, Because he married me before to Romeo?	*cleverly prescribed*
I	To whose foul mouth no healthsome air breathes in, And there die strangled *ere* my Romeo comes.	*before*

1.   Exactly what you think Juliet's *'dismal scene'* is? List.

_____

_____

_____

_____

2.   Juliet is prepared to kill herself rather than marry Paris.
       What words/line in the text reflects this? _____

_____

3.   Given Juliet is ready to kill herself, why do you think she is so full of doubts
       regarding the Friar's 'potion'?

_____

_____

_____

4.   Do you share Juliet's fears and doubts? Why/Why not? _____

_____

_____

5.   If you were Juliet, would you drink the potion? Why/Why not? _____

_____

_____

6.   Do you think such a 'potion' really exists? _____

7.   Do you think there was some form of anaesthetic in Shakespeare's time that
       'resembled' death?

_____

8.   Why do you think Juliet is not being honest and truthful in telling her parents
       of her marriage to Romeo?

_____

_____

_____

9.   Do you think that Juliet is being cowardly in not facing up to her actions?
       Why/Why not?

_____

_____

18A   O WOEFUL DAY

[Act IV, Scene 5]   The Nurse

1.   Read the text quickly: *Who is dead?*
2.   Put the words [in the box] into the text.
3.   In pairs, compare your answers.
4.   Listen. Complete and check your answers.

wake	clothes	~~word~~	asleep	black
Lady	week	wake	forgive	bed

Mistress what mistress, Juliet, *fast* I warrant her she,   *fast asleep*
Why lamb, why Lady, fie you *slug-a-bed*,   *lazy person*
Why love I say, Madam, sweet-heart, why Bride:
What not a __word__ , you take *your pennyworths* now,   *what little you can get*
Sleep for a _____, for the next night I *warrant*   *guarantee*
The County Paris hath *set up his rest*,   *made up his mind*
That you shall rest but little, God _____ me;
Marry and amen: how sound is she _____:
I needs must _____ her: Madam, Madam, Madam,
Ay, let the County *take* you in your _____,   *find*
He'll *fright you up* i'faith, will it not be?   *Frighten you into getting up*
What dress'd, and in your _____, and *down* again?   *lying down*
I must needs _____ you, Lady, Lady, Lady.
Alas, alas, help, help, my Lady's dead.
O well-a-day that ever I was born,
Some *aqua-vitae* ho, my Lord, my _____.   *['water of life'] liquor*

O *woe*, O *woeful*, woeful, woeful day,   *sorrow / sorrowful*
Most *lamentable* day, most woeful day   *sad & regrettable*
That ever, ever I did yet *behold*.   *see*
O day, O day, O day, O hateful day,
Never was seen so _____ a day as this,
O woeful day, O woeful day.

30

Romeo, Balthasar

1. Read the text quickly: *The Balthasar brings ill news. Regarding whom?*
2. Replace the definitions with Shakespeare's own words [in the box].
3. In pairs, compare your answers.
4. Listen. Complete and check your answers.

reviv'd	presage	pardon
kindred's	immortal	his throne
unaccustom'd	leave	Capels
~~the flattering truth~~	presently took post	but love's shadows

Definitions

Romeo: If I may trust __the flattering truth__ of sleep,   the wish fulfilment
My dreams _____ some joyful news at hand,   predict
My *bosom's Lord* sits lightly in _____: *love* / Romeo's heart
And all this day an _____ spirit,   unusual
Lifts me above the ground with cheerful thoughts.
I dreamt my Lady came and found me dead,
(Strange dream that gives a dead man _____ to think)
And breath'd such life with kisses in my lips,   permission
That I _____ and was an Emperor.   came back to life
Ah me, how sweet is love itself possess'd
When _____ are so rich in joy.   the mere dreams of love

Enter Romeo's man Balthasar

News from Verona, how now Balthasar,
Dost thou not bring me letters from the Friar?
How doth my Lady? Is my father well?
How doth my Lady Juliet? That I ask again,
For nothing can be ill, if she be well.

Man: Then she is well, and nothing can be ill,
Her body sleeps in _____ monument,   Capulet's
And her _____ part with angels lives.   undying
I saw her laid low in her _____ vault,   family's
And _____ to tell it you: immediately set out
O _____ me for bringing these ill news,   forgive

31

Discussion

1.   What do you think *'her immortal part'* is referring to? _____

2.   Do you think that 'dreams' [when we are asleep] have a purpose? Why?

_____

_____

3.   Do you think dreams ...
     (a)   are wish fulfilling [ie reflect your wishes]? Why/Why not?
     (b)   predict/tell the future? Why/Why not?
     (c)   reflect one's fears? Why/Why not?
     (d)   are a means of processing the day's events? Why/Why not?
     (e)   have any significance? Why/Why not?

_____

_____

_____

4.   What type of dream do you think Romeo's dream is? Why?

_____

_____

5.   Why do you think Romeo is cheerful after his dream?

_____

_____

6.   What is the strangest dream you've ever had? What type of dream do you
     think it is? What do you think it meant?

_____

_____

_____

7.   How do you think the story would have unfolded, had Romeo received word
     of the Friar's plan?

_____

_____

_____

_____

8.   Do you think the music complemented the text? Why/Why not?
     How would you have done it?

_____

_____

Romeo

1.   In groups discuss: *Would you be willing to die for love? Why/Why not?*
2.   In groups/pairs, put the text in order.
3.   Listen. Complete and check the order.

A	Come bitter *conduct*, come *unsavoury* guide, Thou desperate pilot, now at once run on The dashing rocks, thy sea-sick weary *bark*:	*guide / unpleasant* *small ship*
B	..........................Ah dear Juliet Why art thou yet so fair? Shall I believe	
C	Thee here in dark to be his *paramour*? For fear of that I still will stay with thee,	*mistress*
D	Here's to my love. O true apothecary: Thy drugs are quick. Thus with a kiss I die.	
E	And never from this palace of dim night Depart again: here, here will I remain, With worms that are thy chamber-maids: O here	
F	Arms take your last embrace: and lips, O you The doors of breath, *seal* with a righteous kiss A *dateless bargain to engrossing** death: **an everlasting contract with monopolising*	*close*
G	Will I set up my everlasting rest: And *shake the yoke* of *inauspicious stars**, From this world-wearied flesh: eyes look your last:	*weaken the bond* **unfavourable fortune*
H	That *unsubstantial* death is *amorous* And that the lean *abhorred* monster keeps	*bodiless / in love* *hated*

33

[Act V, Scene 3]   Juliet and Friar Laurence

1. Read the text carefully and decide who is speaking.
2. Place the words [in the box] into the text.
3. In pairs, compare your answers.
4. Listen. Complete and check your answers.

power	poison	~~Lord~~	die	remember
question	drunk	lips	Romeo	stay
noise	husband	Nuns	cup	kiss

_____: O *comfortable* Friar, where is my **Lord**?   *providing comfort*
             I do _____ well where I should be:
             And there I am, where is my _____?

_____: I hear some _____ Lady, come from that nest
             Of death, *contagion* and unnatural sleep: *infection*
             A greater _____ than we can *contradict*   *oppose*
             Hath *thwarted* our intents, come, come away,   *prevented*
             Thy _____ in thy bosom there lies dead:
             And Paris too: come, I'll dispose of thee,
             Among a Sisterhood of holy _____:
             Stay not to _____, for the watch is coming,
             Come go good Juliet, I dare no longer _____.

_____: Go *get thee hence*, for I will not away.   *begone*
             What's here? A _____ clos'd in my true love's hand?
             Poison I see hath been his *timeless* end: *untimely*
             O *churl*, _____ all? And left no friendly drop   *unmannerly peasant*
             To help me after, I will _____ thy lips,
             Haply some _____ yet doth hang on them,
             To make me _____ with a *restorative*.   *kiss that should have revived me*
             Thy _____ are warm,

             <Enter Boy & Watch>

             Yea noise? Then I'll be brief. O *happy* dagger.   *fortunately placed*
             This is thy *sheath*, there rust and let me die.   *cover for a knife*

The Prince of Verona, Capulet, Montague   [Act V, Scene 3]

1. In groups/pairs a) put the text in order and b) decide who is speaking..
2. Listen. Complete and check the order.

A _____ :	A *glooming* peace this morning with it brings, The Sun for sorrow will not show his head: Go hence to have more talk of these sad things, Some shall be pardon'd, and some punished. For never was a story of more woe, Than this of Juliet and her Romeo.	*gloomy*
B _____ :	As rich shall *Romeo's* by his Lady's lie, Poor *sacrifices* of our *enmity*.	*Romeo's statue* *victims / hostility*
C _____ :	O brother Montague, give me thy hand, This is my daughter's *jointure*, for no more can I demand.	*dowry*
D _____ :	But I can give thee more, For I will raise her statue in pure gold, That whiles Verona by that name in known, There shall no *figure* at such *rate* be set, As that of true and faithful Juliet.	*statue / value*
E _____ :	This letter doth make good the Friar's words, Their course of love, the *tidings* of her death: And here he writes, that he did buy a poison Of a poor 'pothecary, and therewithal, Came to this vault, to die and lie with Juliet. Where be these enemies? Capulet, Montague? See what a *scourge* is laid upon your hate! That heaven finds means to kill your joys with love, And I for winking at your discords too, Have lost *a brace* of kinsmen: all are punish'd.	*news* *devastation* *a pair of*

22B   A Story of Woe [Act V, Scene 3]

Discussion

1.   *'See what a scourge is laid upon your hate!*
     That heaven finds means to kill your joys with love'
     Comment on the Shakespeare's effective use of irony _____

     _____

2.   What do you think the Prince means by: *'And I winking at your discords too'*?

     _____

3.   Who do you think *'a brace of kinsmen'* is referring to?

     _____

4.   Would you describe the ending as a tragic ending or a happy ending?
     Give your reasons.

     _____

     _____

5.   How would you have ended the play? List your options and give your
     reasons for your final choice.

     _____

     _____

6.   Discuss the following. Do you agree/disagree & why.

     Violence is never the solution to anything. _____

     _____

     Prejudice of any kind is destructive. _____

     _____

     You can't help who you fall in love with. _____

     _____

     Enemies have more things in common than differences. _____

     _____

     Violence breeds violence. _____

     _____

     Law and authority are there for a better life for all of us [friends and enemies
     alike]. _____

     _____

1. **art**.................... are
2. **aught**.............. anything
3. **dost/doest**...... do
4. **doth**.................. does
5. **didst**................ did
6. **fair** .... beautiful
7. **hast/hath**........ has
8. **hither** .... here
9. **me thinks**........ I think
10. **nought**............. nothing
11. **presently** .... immediately
12. **thee/thou**.................. you
13. **thee** .... you [pl]
14. **thine** .... yours
15. **thither** ....there
16. **thy** ....your
17. **thyself**...................yourself
18. **wast**............................ was
19. **wench**.............. young girl
20. **wherefore** .... why
21. **wilt** .... will
22. **yonder**...............that there

Refer to above list & transcribe the following into modern English:-

1.   Dost thou live in a fair city? _____

2.   Go thither presently and wait for me. _____

3.   Come hither and finish thy work! _____

4.   Me thinks thou art in love with yonder wench. _____

5.   Is thy school far? _____

6.   Wilt thou go to school in the morrow? _____

7.   Wherefore didst thou not say aught? _____

8.   Wherefore dost thou speak loudly? _____

9.   Wherefore are thou late for school? _____

10. Doth time mean nought to you? _____

11. Get thyself a new jacket. _____

12. He hath bought a new book. _____

13. I thank thee for everything. _____

14. Keep it – it is thine and not mine. _____

Shakespeare-Speak

1. **art**....................... are
2. **aught**................. anything
3. **dost/doest**....... do
4. **doth**................... does
5. **didst**................. did
6. **fair** .... beautiful
7. **hast/hath**......... has
8. **hither** .... here
9. **me thinks**......... I think
10. **nought**............. nothing
11. **presently** .... immediately
12. **thee/thou**................... you
13. **thee** .... you [pl]
14. **thine** .... yours
15. **thither** ....there
16. **thy** ....your
17. **thyself**..................yourself
18. **wast**............................. was
19. **wench**..............young girl
20. **wherefore** .... why
21. **wilt** .... will
22. **yonder**..............that there

Refer to above list & transcribe the following into 'Shakespearean' English:-

1.   Do you have a girl/boyfriend? _____

2.   Go there immediately and see if he's alone. _____

3.   Come here you beautiful girl! _____

4.   I think s/he's beautiful; do you? _____

5.   What is your name? _____

6.   Won't you come to the cinema? _____

7.   Why did you speak to him? _____

8.   Why do you ask so many questions? _____

9.   Why are you sad? _____

10. Does my hair look beautiful? _____

11. Get yourself ready to go out. _____

12. He has asked me out. _____

13. Thank you for nothing! _____

14. She's a beautiful girl! _____

Sentence completion activities incorporate the multi-skill approach of reading, writing and listening.

The above activities are aimed at improving SS general language abilities and increasing SS awareness of elements that make up a coherent text that also serves them in their writing. The activities aim to develop a stronger awareness of how rules of grammar, style, punctuation and lexis play a part in that process.

It is imperative that SS are given clear instructions & examples so that they can grasp the purpose of the activity and hence enjoy the activity.

How to help Students:
SS might feel despondent at not being able to complete sentences in their own words.
- Incorporate a 'simple' warmer activity [see plan] to familiarise SS with the following collaboration activity.
- Make SS aware that it's a collaborative exercise; akin to a puzzle that they have to complete.
- Emphasise the importance of meaning and association of ideas.

SS might 'mishear' words.
- Remind them of the context and encourage them to think of other plausible words [given the context].

SS may experience difficulty with reference to unknown vocabulary.
- Ensure vocabulary is covered:-
  Either pre-teach [via SS exchanging known definitions/matching exercises/illuminating sentences]
  Or clarify any vague/non essential vocabulary towards the end [feedback stage].
- Provide difficult vocabulary on the W/B as clues to assist SS.

SS might produce correct sentences [albeit not what is in the text/played].
- If the sentence is grammatically & contextually correct, accept as such. However, on feedback, provide the actual text.

GUIDANCE NOTES
Gap-fill Activities

Gap-fill activities are aimed at improving SS general language abilities and increasing SS awareness of elements that make up a coherent text that also serves them in their writing. The activities aim to develop a stronger awareness of how rules of grammar, style, punctuation and lexis play a part in that process.

It is imperative that SS are given clear instructions & examples so that they can grasp the purpose of the activity and hence enjoy the activity.

How to help Students:

SS might feel despondent at having to take on board unfamiliar vocabulary, reading and incorporating words into the text and listening.

- Ensure that you follow the activity in clear stages.
- Ensure SS read the whole text before attempting to fill any gaps.
- Tell SS to look for 'clues' and pay particular attention to sentence structure, punctuation, word types and reference markers.
- Tell SS to be constantly aware of meaning and the association of ideas.
- Point out the logic of elimination.
- Ensure that SS are not overloaded in the activity by shortening and changing the exercise to suit your SS needs & level.
- Emphasise that guessing the gaps is just as important and not to be afraid of mistakes.

SS might mishear or not catch words.

- Remind them of the context and encourage them to think of other plausible words [given the context].

SS may experience difficulty with reference to unknown vocabulary.

- Ensure vocabulary is covered via vocabulary boxes that permit SS to deduce meaning from context for themselves.
- Clarify any vague/abstract vocabulary towards the end [feedback stage].

SS might produce correct words in gaps, albeit not what is in the actual text.

- Encourage SS to use logic/elimination.
- If the sentence is grammatically & contextually correct, accept as such. However, on feedback, provide the actual text.

Text Ordering collaborative activities are aimed at improving SS general language abilities and increasing SS awareness of elements that make up a coherent text that also serves them in their writing. The activities actively engage SS to look for meaning and association of ideas in a given text whilst increasing awareness of contextual clues, ie, grammatical cues [cohesive devices, reference markers, conjunctions/linking words, lexical substitution], punctuation, rhyme and style.

It is imperative that SS are given clear instructions & examples so that they can grasp the purpose of the activity and hence enjoy the activity.

How to help Students:
SS might feel frustrated/daunted at the difficulty of the task.
- Ensure that you follow the activity in clear stages.
- Make SS aware that it's a collaborative exercise; akin to a puzzle that they have to put together.
- Tell SS to look for clues and pay particular attention to sentence structure, punctuation, word types and reference markers.
- Tell SS to be constantly aware of meaning and the association of ideas.
- Ensure that SS are not overloaded in the activity by shortening and altering the exercise to suit your SS needs & level.
- Emphasise that it is fundamentally a listening activity and that the activity merely serves to assist/help by familiarising them with the text.

SS might mishear or not catch phrases/text.
- Remind them of the context and encourage them to think of other plausible words/phrases [given the context].
- Repeat listening as required.

SS may experience difficulty with reference to unknown vocabulary.
- Ensure vocabulary is covered via vocabulary boxes that permit SS to deduce meaning from context for themselves.
- Clarify any vague/abstract vocabulary towards the end [feedback stage].

SS may find the text too vague to associate with anything concrete.
- Ensure that you outline the scene from the play & provide some form of concrete context before the activity.
- Incorporate essential vocabulary/theme questions as warmer.

Book: <u>R &J: The Concert</u>   Guidance Notes: <u>Page: 39-41</u>
Title: <u>   </u>   Tutor: <u>   </u>
Date::   <u>   </u>   Class: <u>   </u>

READING   (Approx 15 minutes)

Overall Aims:

to familiarise SS with the text, worksheet and vocabulary.

to provide SS time to absorb the general meaning of the text.

to provide practice in reading for gist.

to provide reading practice in scanning for specific information.

to provide detailed reading practice for better understanding of the text.

to increase awareness of meaning and association of ideas in a given context.

to allow SS time to decode difficult vocabulary.

Procedure	Aims
T hands out the worksheet	- to provide SS with a hard copy for reference - to allow familiarization with the worksheet
(a) T asks SS to read quickly & find out who is speaking	- to provide SS with motivation/reason for reading - to develop SS skills in reading for gist
(b) T asks SS to read quickly & answer a specific question [i.e. How many hours long is the play?]	- to provide SS with motivation/reason for reading - to develop SS reading skills in scanning for specific information
(c) T asks SS to read and find out who is speaking in the given dialogue	- to provide SS with detailed reading practice - to increase awareness of meaning, association of ideas and sequences within a given text
Class feedback.	- to check and assess comprehension
T asks SS for definitions of given words in italics [select accordingly] T clarifies with examples (elicited from SS)	- Further practice in scanning for specific information - to allow familiarization with text and vocabulary - to allow SS time to decode difficult vocabulary - to prepare SS for the ensuing vocabulary exercise - to clarify and ensure understanding of given vocabulary

VOCABULARY (Approx 10 minutes)

Overall Aims: to teach/pre-teach difficult words via encouraging SS to think and deduce meaning of words for themselves.

to enable better understanding of the text.

to provide detailed reading practice.

to develop SS skills in making use of given contextual and grammatical clues.

Procedure	Aims
T asks SS to complete the vocabulary exercise: (a) Matching words to definitions and/or (b) Putting words into the text	- to pre-teach unfamiliar vocabulary - to develop SS skills deduction and elimination - to develop SS skills in recognising word types - to develop SS skills in making use of contextual and grammatical clues [i.e. capitalization] - to develop SS skills in deducing meaning from context
T asks SS in pairs to compare their answers	- to allow SS time to compare and discuss differences - to allow T to monitor and assess comprehension
SS check via listening	Follow on: LISTENING [Page: 47]

Optional Procedure	Aims

T selects/lists words on w/b
T asks SS to individually mark the words they
 	
  ✓ know
  ✗ don't know
  ? not sure
	- to teach/pre-teach vocabulary
	- to activate known knowledge
	- to highlight unknown knowledge

In groups SS explain words they know to each other Groups then exchange what they know with each other	- to develop SS skills in providing definitions - to allow SS to discuss/explain to each other - to encourage SS to recognise word types - to encourage SS to guess/deduce from context - to allow T to monitor and assess comprehension
T provides explanations and/or illuminating sentences, SS have to figure out which word it refers to	- to encourage SS to think and deduce meaning of words for themselves - to check comprehension and clarify

TEXT ORDERING (Approx 15 minutes)

Overall Aims: to provide SS with practice in sequencing a coherent text.

to actively engage SS to look for meaning and association of ideas in a given text.

to actively engage SS to look for grammatical clues within a given text.

Procedure	Aims
Optional	VOCABULARY [Page: 44] Optional Procedure
T asks SS to sit in groups T outlines the scene T explains the task T hands out the jumbled text to each group	- to set up the collaborative activity - to provide them with a context - to prepare SS for the ensuing activity
SS in groups collaborate and organise the given text	- to allow SS interaction and collaboration - to allow exchange of information/ideas - to increase awareness of sentence structure - to increase awareness of text cohesion - to encourage SS to look for grammatical clues [in terms of cohesive devices: reference markers, conjunctions/linking words; lexical substitution] - to increase awareness of meaning/logic and association of ideas - to increase awareness of rhyme and style
T monitors and assists.	- to allow T to assess comprehension and problem areas and to assist SS by reminding them of the above
SS check via listening	Follow on: LISTENING [Page: 47]

SENTENCE COMPLETION (Approx 15 minutes)

Overall Aims: to provide SS with practice in listening for specific information.
to actively engage SS to look for meaning and association of ideas.
to actively engage SS to look for grammatical clues to complete sentences.

Procedure	Aims
Optional	VOCABULARY [Page: 44] Optional Procedure
T writes on w/b: *a) I bought _____.* *b) It went well with <u>my red shoes</u>.* T elicits various options from SS and concept checks with erroneous suggestions, i.e. *I bought <u>a house/ computer/ book</u>* T writes options on w/b: a) <u>*a red dress*</u>/ *some icecream/ some salad/ a new lipstick/ some grapes* b) <u>*my red shoes*</u>/ *cheese/ my skin tone/ steak/ the apple pie* T instructs pairs to produce as many correct variations to complete the sentences. T elicits and accepts all correct variations.	- to set up the ensuing activity - to provide SS with a framework - to prepare SS for the ensuing activity - to allow SS interaction and collaboration - to allow exchange of information/ideas - to highlight the importance of meaning and association of ideas. - to highlight awareness of sentence structure - to highlight importance of grammatical clues - to highlight flexibility and purpose of ensuing activity - to avoid SS becoming despondent [at not being able to complete sentences in their own words]
T hands out top half of the worksheet only and instructs SS, in pairs, to complete the sentences.	- to familiarize SS with the context - to encourage SS to look for meaning, association of ideas and grammatical clues - to allow SS interaction and collaboration
Preliminary Listening: T instructs SS to listen and find out if their sentences are close to actual words.	- to provide SS practice in listening for specific information - to provide SS with the opportunity to compare the given text with their own sentences.
	Follow on: LISTENING [Page: 47]

LISTENING   (Approx 5-10 minutes)

Overall Aims: to allow SS to complete/check their answers via listening practice

to develop skills in listening for specific information

to develop skills in intensive listening and note taking

Procedure	Aims
T instructs SS to listen and depending on the exercise: (i) check their answers (ii) check their text order (iii) complete the sentences	- to clarify the aim of the ensuing listening activity **Note: Distinguishing between male characters in the listening is very difficult. Therefore, draw SS attention to content. Elicit correct characters and clarify.**
Listening (1): SS complete/check their answers, text order, or complete the sentences	- to allow SS to complete/check their answers Depending on the exercise:- - to provide practice in intensive listening and/or - to provide practice in listening for specific information
Pairs compare answers T monitors and assists	- to allow SS interaction and collaboration - to allow the exchange of information/opinion
T repeats Listening (1) if necessary/required Class feedback	- to allow SS to check/listen for any 'misheard' words - to allow SS more time to complete the activity - to ensure comprehension and clarify any problems
Listening (2): SS listen for enjoyment	- to aid memory retention
Optional	VOCABULARY [Page: 44] Optional Procedure
Unfinished Sentences:- T hands out bottom half of the worksheet or expands activity via dictation	- to provide SS with a hard copy for reference - to provide SS with further practice of listening, reading and writing
Optional	Follow on: SPEAKING [Page: 48]

SPEAKING   (Approx 20-30 minutes)

Overall Aims: to provide SS with speaking practice/discussion points to better understand the text

to develop speaking skills in: expressing opinions

agreeing/disagreeing

Procedure	Aims
T hands out worksheet	- to provide SS with a hard copy - to encourage note-taking
In groups SS go through the worksheet; discuss; exchange opinions and take notes. T monitors/assists.	- to ensure comprehension of text - to further initiate SS interest in the text via expanding the themes - to allow SS to better relate to the text via personalised questions - to provide SS with speaking practice - to provide SS with note taking practice - to develop SS skills in expressing opinions - to develop SS skills in agreeing and disagreeing - to allow SS interaction - to enhance group dynamics
Class feedback	- to summarise and close the activity with interest

WRITING   (Approx 10 minutes)

Overall Aims: to provide SS with writing practice

to develop SS writing skills in: transcription

word substitution

Procedure	Aims
T hands out worksheet	- to provide SS with a hard copy - to encourage note-taking
In groups SS transcribe the text into modern day language [or vise versa] T monitors/assists Class feedback	- to initiate SS interest by relating the text to the here and now [and vise versa] - to allow SS to discuss and exchange opinions - to provide SS with writing practice - to close the activity with interest

01 Prologue [Chorus] Page: 01

A: (1) Two hours.

(2) lay, mutiny, civil, From forth, star-cross'd, misadventur'd, strife, passage, rage, nought, toil.

B: (3) Suggested Pros: acts as a reminder not to forget/happen again, ensures others are aware/wary and don't forget/allow to happen again.

Suggested Cons: poisonous, makes you bitter/resentful, inflexible, doesn't allow for realization/acknowledgment of errors/forgiveness.

02 Rebellious Subjects [Act I, Scene 1] Page: 03

A: (1) This afternoon.

(2) profaners, pernicious, issuing, mistemper'd, moved, brawls, thrice, Cast by, To wield, forfeit, pleasure, common.

B: (1) Suggestions: Rebellious, enemies, profaners, neighbour-stained, beasts, fire, pernicious rage, purple fountains, issuing from veins, bloody hands, mistemper'd weapons, canker'd with peace, canker'd hate.

(6) Suggested Pros: appropriate punishment, eye for an eye justice, sets an example, acts as deterrent, no prison costs, guarantees public safety.

Suggested Cons: immoral, playing god, wrong convictions, irreversible, no real compensation for loss, vengeful.

03 The Feast of Capulet [Act I, Scene 2] Page: 05

A: (1) Benvolio, Romeo, Benvolio, Romeo.

(2) *devout*-deeply felt, *unattainted*-unprejudiced, *feast*-party, *crow*-a black bird, *sups*-dines, *pois'd with*-balanced against, *match*-equal, *splendour*-beauty, *rejoice*-be happy, *scant*-hardly, *heretics*-non-believers.

(3) feast, sups, unattainted, crow, devout, heretics, match, pois'd with, scant, rejoice, splendour.

B: (1) Suggestions: untainted eye, devout religion of mine eye, maintains such falsehood, turn tears to fires, transparent heretics, all-seeing Sun, herself poised with herself in either eye, crystal scales, these who often drown'd.

(2) *these* - Romeo's eyes, *drown'd* - cried (re Rosalind's rejection of him), *transparent heretics* - Romeo's eyes.

(3) *crystal scales* - Romeo's eyes.

04 Gentle Sin [Act I, Scene 5] Page: 07

A: 1(c), 2(a), 3(d), 4(f), 5(e), 6(h), 7(b), 8(g).

B: (2) Text order: 1:E, 2:B, 3:I, 4:H, 5:A, 6:F, 7:C, 8:D, 9:G.

C: (1) Suggestions: *profane, prayer* - touch/*holy shrine* - Juliet/*blushing pilgrims* - lips/*sin, my prayer's effect* - kiss.

(2) *this holy shrine* -Juliet.

(3) *this* - holding her hand.

(4) *do what hands do* - touch/kiss.

(5) *my prayers effect* -my prayers fulfillment.

(6) kiss 1: after *Then move not while...* & before *Thus from my lips, by thine ...*
kiss 2: after *Give me my sin again.*

05 Juliet is the Sun [Act II, Scene 2] Page: 10

A: (1) Romeo.

   (2) Box A: light, East, moon, pale, envious, fools, Lady, nothing, answer, speaks.

       Box B: heaven, eyes, twinkle, brightness, daylight, bright, birds, cheek, glove, touch.

06 Take All Myself [Act II, Scene 2] Page: 11

A: (2) Text order: 1:K, 2:I, 3:Q, 4:B, 5:J, 6:L, 7:H, 8:E, 9:P, 10:F, 11:C, 12:M, 13:O, 14:D, 15:G, 16:N, 17:A.

B: (1) Why are you [named] Romeo?/Be as perfect as he is./Get rid of your name.

07 Two in One [Act II, Scene 6] Page: 13

A: (1) Wedding/marriage.

   (2) Friar, Romeo, Friar, Juliet, Friar, Juliet, Romeo, Juliet, Friar.

B: (1) Suggestions: could be reflecting on the Friar's experience that some people regret getting married later in life, that those who rush into marriage/who do not obtain their parent's consent regret getting married in later years or perhaps he has a premonition based on the families long lasting feud.

   (2) Going too fast is as bad as going too slow.

   (3) Marriage/wedding.

   (4) Before *Here comes the Lady.....* Romeo kisses her. Juliet kissed him back.

   (5) Marriage proposal.

   (6) (a) *Conceit more rich in matter than in words, brags of his substance, not of ornament:*

       (b) *They are but beggars that can count their worth,*

08 Plague on Both Houses [Act III, Scene 1] Page: 15

A: (1) (a) Text Order: 1:F, 2:C, 3:G, 4:E, 5:D, 6:B, 7:I, 8:H, 9:A.

       (b) (1) Romeo, (2) <*Tybalt under...*>, (3) Mercutio, (4) Benvolio, (5) Mercutio, (6) Romeo, (7) Mercutio, (8) Romeo, (9) Mercutio.

09 Fortune's Fool [Act III, Scene 1] Page: 17

A: (1) (a) Text Order: 1:D, 2:A, 3:G, 4:E, 5:B, 6:F, 7:H, 8:C, 9:J, 10:I.

       (b) (1) Romeo, (2) Benvolio, (3) Romeo, (4) Benvolio, (5) Romeo, (6) Tybalt, (7) Romeo, (8) <*They fight...*>, (9) Romeo, (10) Benvolio.

B: (2) Suggestions: This but begins, the woe others must end/Away to heaven, respective lenity/fire and fury, be my conduct now/Staying for thine to keep him company/Either thou or I, or both, must go with him.

11 Back Foolish Tears [Act III, Scene 2] Page: 20

A: (1) Juliet.

   (2) Box 1: *native*-source.origin, *tributary*-paid as tribute, *drops*-tears, *woe*-sorrow, *weep*-cry, *deeds*-actions, *fain*-gladly, *banished*-exiled.

   (3) Box 2: Lord, wife, cousin, cousin, husband, husband, Tybalt, Tybalt, husband, Tybalt, Tybalt, Romeo, Tybalts, Tybalt.

12 Verona Walls [Act III, Scene 3] Page: 21

A: (1) *without*-outside, *torture*-causing strong pain as punishment, *banished*-exiled, *stroke*-movement of arm, *mis-termed*-misnamed, *mercy*-forgiveness.

(2) Text order: 1:C, 2:I, 3:G, 4:K, 5:F, 6:A, 7:L, 8:B, 9:D, 10:H, 11:J. 12:E.

13 There Art Thou Happy [Act III, Scene 3] Page: 22

A: (1) The Friar.

(2) Box 1: *denote*-indicate, *unseemly*-improper, *disposition*-nature, *temper'd*-balanced, *slay/slew/slain*-kill, *rouse*-make angry.

(3) Box 2: hand, man, womanish, beast, Tyblat, Lady, thyself, Juliet, kill, happy.

B: (1) <*Romeo offers to stab himself and the nurse snatches the dagger away*>

(2 & 3) killing oneself

(6) Suggestions: Art thou a man?/Thy tears are womanish/unreasonable fury of a beast/unseemly woman in a seeming man/ill-beseeming beast in seeming both/thou hast amaz'd me/by doing damned hate upon yourself/like a misbehav'd and sullen wench.

14 Let's Talk [Act III, Scene 5] Page: 24

A: (1) (a) Text order: 1:D, 2:C, 3:B, 4:A.

(b) (1) Juliet, (2) Romeo, (3) Juliet, (4) Romeo.

B: (1) the moon.

(2) He will forfeit his life (as decreed by the The Prince)

(3) To have him stay with her a while longer.

(4) Encourages him to leave.

15 I Will Not Marry Paris [Act III, Scene 5] Page: 25

A: (1) Juliet's father.

B: (1) Paris.

(3) Suggestions: My fingers/hands are restless, have a impulsive/instinctive urge.

(9) Suggested transcription:
Go hang yourself/Forget about you/To hell with you/Get lost,
you worthless girl/hussy/whore/prostitute,
I'll tell you what, get yourself to church on Thursday
Or never look me in the face again.
Don't say anything, don't reply, don't talk back to me.
I feel like slapping you. Wife, we never thought ourselves blessed/lucky,
That God only gave us this one child,
But now I see that this one is one too many.
And that we were cursed when we had her.
Send her out, the little hussy/the good for nothing/the worthless piece of trash.

16 Like Death [Act IV, Scene 1] Page: 27
A: (1) Mantua.
    (2) home, marry, alone, Nurse, drink, cold, breath, cheeks, ashes, death, forty, sleep, Bridegroom, bed, robes, letters, waking, free, shame.

17 What If [Act IV, Scene 3] Page: 28
A: (2) Text order: 1:G, 2:F, 3:A, 4:D, 5:H, 6:B, 7:E, 8:I, 9:C.
B: (1) Suggestions: Married Romeo without her parents knowledge/consent;
           is due to marry Paris tomorrow and hence commit (the crime of) bigamy;
           is about to drink a potion that might end her life.
    (2) No, this shall forbid it, lie thou there. *<laying down the dagger>*.

18 O Woeful Day [Act IV, Scene 5] Page: 30
A: (1) Juliet.
    (2) word, week, forgive, asleep, wake, bed, clothes, wake, Lady, black.

19 Ill News [Act V, Scene 1] Page: 31
A: (1) Juliet
    (2) the flattering truth, presage, his throne, unaccustom'd, leave, reviv'd, but love's shadows, Capel's, immortal, kindred's, presently took post, pardon.
B: (1) her spirit/soul.

20 Here Will I Remain [Act V, Scene 3] Page: 33
A: (2) Text order: 1:B, 2:H, 3:C, 4:E, 5:G, 6:F, 7:A, 8:D.

21 Kiss Thy Lips [Act V, Scene 3] Page: 34
A: (1) Juliet, Friar, Juliet.
    (2) Lord, remember, Romeo, noise, power, husband, Nuns, question, stay, cup, drunk, kiss, poison, die, lips.

22 A Story of Woe [Act V, Scene 3] Page: 35
A: (1) (a) Text order: 1:E, 2:C, 3:D, 4:B, 5:A.
       (b) (1) Prince, (2) Capulet, (3) Montague, (4) Capulet, (5) Prince.
B: (2) not taking it seriously enough.
    (3) Romeo & Paris.

ABOUT THE AUTHOR

www.doubledutchdiscords.com

INDEX OF EXERCISES

Made in the USA
Charleston, SC
06 December 2013